# COMMUNICATION FOR SURVIVAL

Volume One. It Didn't Have to End So/
It Could Have Ended Differently

## Eugenia Springer

**ESProductions**

Createspace ISBN:9781482635041
Personal ISBN: 976-95058-5-4
Contact EugeniaSpringer Productions at journeybooks43@gmail.com

Cover design by Docu Center, Newtown, Trinidad and Tobago, Courtesy,
Jacqueline Kitson

Printed in the United States of America

*Dedicated*
*To*
*all peoples of my beloved homeland,*
*Trinidad & Tobago*

# INTRODUCTION

In this book, *Communication for Survival/It Didn't Have to End So*, I present two versions of nine different stories.

These stories are all fictional, but they are built around similar incidents occurring too often, in my beloved home country, Trinidad and Tobago.

All characters are fictitious.

Each story in the first version turns out unpleasantly or tragically.

In the second version of each story I change the communication style and so modify the outcome of the story.

You are familiar with these stories. They are daily played out among us in our various countries and hometowns.

Read and judge for yourself.

It takes just one person in any disagreement, to respond in a way that defuses explosive, confrontational energies. All around, people are hurting. They want relief. Let's listen, to understand how they are feeling. Let's listen to them even when they are blaming us; even when we don't agree with what they are saying.

Ego would push us to to fight back, to defend our self. But what if instead of distressing our self with rage, we allow our self to listen to what the person is expressing. Shift our focus from being vexed, to listening to how the person is feeling.

I am committed to responding to everyone compassi onately, and empathically. You can join me. Love is a healing emotion. Join me as I commit myself to relating to every person, lovingly. Let us relate to others as we would want them to relate to us. Together, we can make the environment around us, a space in which anyone would like to linger.

Everyone wants to be heard. Everyone wants to be understood, Everyone wants to know that how they feel matters; that someone cares. As we pay attention to those who are trying to be heard, we are helping them realize that life is a gift they can cherish.

What I am asking of you, and demanding of myself, takes work. What matters is that we practice what we teach.

We want others to be perfect, then let us practice doing the right thing at all times. And when we behave in ways we are not proud of, let us be big hearted enough to acknowledge what we did, if another is involved, and try again.

We can all be big hearted. Let's make our self smile pleasantly and allow others the freedom to correct themselves when they slip up, rather than show anger and blame.

As you and I follow **The Golden Rule**, we feel better, and we help others to feel better. Here is **the Golden Rule**:

*"Relate to others as you would like others to relate to you."*

*Empathy and compassion dissolve hostility. Where compassion dwells, anger is not accommodated. When anger is absent, joy feels at home. Where joy is, love appears. And they both--love and joy, always settle at Peace. Everyone can enjoy interacting with a soul at Peace.  No hang-ups, no tension. Great vibes, open-armed acceptance. Visitors to the place of Peace and Joy feel comfortable. If they have something to say, they are listened to. Here, everyone feels special, accepted, and respected. Communication flows smoothly when you are at Peace.*

THE AUTHOR

# CONTENTS

# STORY #1

# Not Worth It

◆ ◆ ◆

"Hey Ma, I'm just going down to the corner for a little bit."

"Boy, I keep telling you this neighborhood changed since you've been away. That corner down there is trouble."

"I'll be okay, Ma. I just have to collect a debt from a brother."

"Lloyd, be careful. After all these years you spent away, I don't want to lose you to these trigger happy people out there."

"Ma, don't worry. I'll be all right. The brother promised me he'd have my money for sure today."

"I wish you had never given that man any money. Look how long he promising to give you back your money. Every time it's another run around, another *cock and bull story*.

"I'm telling you, Lloyd, that man is trouble."

"Give your son a hug, Ma. I'll be back in a little bit."

"Bring me some mints—power mints, please."

"You have it. I love you, Ma."

◆ ◆ ◆

"Hey man, what's up?"

"Cool, man Lloyd, cool."

"Hey brother, you see Screecher?"

"Yes brother. Look, he is right across there by the drugstore with them other brothers."

"Hey Screecher . . . Man, what's up?"

"Cool man, Lloyd. I just here hanging out with my partners."

"Man, you have my money?"

"O Lord, brother, you know I had your money. I had all your money . . ."

"What you mean you had all my money? If you had my money why didn't you bring it to me? When you wanted to borrow my money you didn't have any problem finding me! What kind of scheme you trying on me here? You can't give me my money but you could be wearing eight hundred dollars' sneakers, and new threads?"

"Aye man, cool it, you can't talk to we *pardner* like that."

"Oh? I can't? And who is going to stop me?"

"It's okay brothers. Lloyd and I cool, man. He and I could handle this. We *does go down good.*"

"So what is this, Screecher? You bring your partners and them with you because you know I coming for my money today? You think I'm afraid of your partners?"

"*Nah* man, Lloyd. We just *chillin* here."

"You *chillin* here in your new threads and brand-name sneakers when you know you're supposed to pay me back my three hundred dollars today?"

"Man, I feel real bad about this, but I telling you the god truth . . . Aye man, Lloyd, let go my arm. Man, you twisting my arm. Man, you can't do that, man, Lloyd. You can't twist my arm. Man, my mother didn't have anything to eat, so man, I used your money to put some groceries and market goods in her kitchen."

"And what you want my mother to eat? Eh? Look, give me my money or I'll break this arm behind here, right now!"

"O Lord, man Lloyd. This don't have to go down so, man. I have your money. I will get it for you."

"Come on, you're going to give me every cent you owe me plus interest, right now. Where is my money, you blasted schemer!"

"Aye, let go the man, Lloyd."

"You want to come and make me let him go? Eh *pardner*?"

"You breaking my hand, Lloyd. Don't bend my arm so hard."

"Kick off them sneakers, Screecher, and tell your partners and them to back off, if you want to be able to use this arm again."

"I can't give you my sneakers, man! You can't get my sneakers. I'll get your three hundred for you."

"I'll break this arm right off, you lying-mouth, no-good scamp. I will break this arm off right now if you don't take off those sneakers right now and give them to me. Those sneakers for my money! Now! And *allyuh* partners, don't even try reaching in your pocket if you have plans to go back home today. Kick off them sneakers, Screecher!

Good. Now, get out of here, and don't ever try to borrow money from me again!"

"Aye, look how Lloyd have Screecher barefoot out here. And he just chuck off the man like the man is some little child. He bring down we *pardner*, man. We can't let him treat the man so."

"But you can't take my sneakers, man, Lloyd. You can't take my sneakers! At least let me go home and get some other shoes. You can't leave me barefoot like this out here in the public!"

"Watch me, Screecher. I will sell these and get back my three hundred dollars with interest!"

"Aye Screech, we can't let this go down so, man. The man make you look like a little child. Look how he *have* you out here barefoot. He bring you down real low, man."

"I *ent* letting this pass so, man. Lloyd didn't have any right bringing me down like that. Aye *allyuh*, go home. I taking care of this myself."

"Mr. Druggist, give me two dollars' worth of mint, please."

"For your mother, Lloyd?"

"Yes, Mr. Julien."

"Then it would be power mints. That is all she buys. Here is your mint, Lloyd. And look, take a piece of advice from me. Watch your back. After what just happened out there, you are not safe 'round here—not for one minute. I'm talking to you from experience, eh Lloyd, from experience, boy. How many years you've been away from this country, Lloyd?"

"A long time, Mr. Druggist—since I was a teenager."

"Where were you?"

"In one of the central mountain states in the U.S."

"Boy, I don't know how people settle disputes in that place where you spent all those years, but things changed around here, Lloyd. *Fellahs* around here don't settle disputes with a twist arm, or a clout at the back of the head, anymore. That was how it used to be when you left the country, but things different now."

"You mean they pelt stone and bottle, Mr. Druggist?"

"They don't even pelt stone or bottle again, man Lloyd. Things changed a lot since you went away. Listen to me, watch your back."

"I'm not afraid of these *fellahs*, Mr. Druggist. I could take on all of them anytime they're ready."

"It's not like that anymore, Lloyd. Men don't fight like men used to, long time."

"What you mean, Mr. Druggist?"

"They don't stand up and fight anymore. They only come out to kill these days."

"Yeh? Well, I'll like to see any of them come up to my face to kill me. Let them try. I could take care of myself, Mr. Julien."

"Lloyd, these *fellahs* don't fight like men. They don't live long enough to be men. They will try to get you when you're not looking. They don't give you a chance to defend yourself. These *fellahs* don't have any respect for honor, or life, you know."

"You mean they fight like cowards?"

"Yes. They fight like real cowards, and like frightened, spiteful children. They don't give a man a fighting chance. They peep, and hit, and run."

"Well, I'll handle those little boys when the time comes. See you around, Mr. Julien."

"Mr. Julien, these people slack eh? You mean more than five hours now since the man's body lying here on the ground and they can't move him to the morgue yet? They have the man's body, and this big crowd, in front your drugstore all this time?"

"I just heard from the police, Sam. They just got on to the District Medical Officer. The man was with his family at some beach all evening. They say he was just getting into bed when they finally reached him. But he is leaving now to come."

"Lord, I wonder if there is another country where a body has to stay on the ground till the medical doctor orders them to move it."

"A crying shame, Sam—a crying shame. My whole chest in pain. So many years Lloyd lived abroad. Now he is dead because of a boy half his age. He come back here trying to be friendly to everybody. And look who he found himself close to—a *wotless* boy who is a no-good thief. Look, Lloyd didn't even have time to put the mints in his pocket. And the sneakers he lost his life over, gone."

"People saying Screecher snatched the sneakers and ran off. Lord, I don't know what my country is coming to. A man lost his life over some sneakers? Funerals are so commonplace these days, Mr. Julien."

"This would be one big funeral, more because of Lloyd's mother. How Screecher could shoot the lady's one child? And he playing he running from the police."

"These little no-good boys *does* do their crime then run and hide."

"I know. But man, Sam, it didn't have to end so. It could have ended differently."

## *Story #1. Ending Differently*

Very discreetly, Lloyd goes quietly to Screecher, and whispers in his ear, "Could I see you for a minute, man?"

Given the climate out there I would hope Screecher does not take this invitation as cause *to reach for something.*

Anyhow, they both step aside, a little distance from Screecher's friends.

"Man Screecher, what about that three hundred dollars? I need my money now, man."

Let's say Screecher has absolutely no intention of paying back Lloyd his money, so he stalls again for the umpteenth time.

"O Lord, brother, you know I had your money but I just, just used it. You see, man, my mother didn't have anything to eat, so man, I used your money to put some groceries and market goods in her kitchen."

Let's say the two men look each other in the eye.

Screecher is wearing such an honest expression he would convince any pious soul he is surely telling the truth. But Lloyd, who wants his money, knows the man is *lying through his teeth.*

So Lloyd talks to himself. He thinks, "This man is making me mad. I feel like collaring him here and now, and twisting his arm till he gives me my money.

"Look at these fine threads he's wearing, and look at these eight hundred dollars' sneakers on his feet. I could demand payment in kind, and confiscate his name brand sneakers. But that wouldn't make any sense. It might just make him behave *ignorant*."

Meanwhile Screecher's partners are keeping their eyes on Lloyd. And Lloyd and Screecher are silently looking into each other's eyes.

Screecher is apprehensive, but he is watching the man, and he sees no sign of immediate danger.

"I could set it up so somebody could take care of him for me", Lloyd is thinking, "but I would have to pay out more money to get that done. Furthermore, for the rest of my life I would have to be wondering who found out.

"And if it gets out that I had anything to do with it, then my life gone down the drain. And for what? For this simple man standing here *lying through his teeth* to me.

"Man, this matter with Screecher is not worth the trouble.

"I will waste my life because a poor man is so poor he would lie about three hundred dollars? Man, I'm not throwing away my life for fifty thousand dollars, not for a million, much less for just three hundred dollars."

All that took less than a minute. It was a long time for Screecher, who had his weapon on him. He would have to move fast if Lloyd launched an attack.

But Lloyd was opting for forgiveness.

He was pulling himself out of this situation he found himself in with Screecher.

"Look, partner, that's okay. Whenever you get the three hundred dollars, you could give me."

Screecher's partners relax. They shift their body weight so that they no longer seem ready to lunge at the man staring down their partner's face.

Lloyd, who all this time has them in full focus within his peripheral vision, misses none of this. "Or, you know what", Lloyd says, "you could give me twenty every week, until you pay me off. How is that?"

"Cool, boss, cool. That sounds good. You would get your money, man. Yeh."

And the man, who had just left his mother at home, went into the drugstore and purchased some mints for her, and went back to her home to spend the rest of their lives together.

If Screecher should turn up with the money, Lloyd would be glad. If he doesn't, Lloyd would leave it alone.

So Lloyd did not die foolishly out there in front the drugstore because he took offense at a man who owed him what could have been forgiven, or what could have been arranged in easy payments.

Further, the District Medical Officer did not have to be interrupted just as he was getting into bed for the evening.

And all the people who gathered outside the funeral parlor did not have to be traumatized for yet another time because of another senseless crime.

The community breathed easily that day.

Commuters traveling uninterruptedly to their various destinations were unaware of how close they had come to yet another traffic jam because of another crime-generated funeral procession.

But the real winner in all this was the country of Trinidad and Tobago, which did not have to register that day, another death due to violence.

# Prelude to Story #2

Let's revisit another tragedy, so I could change the tone of the interaction and possibly save a life.

When we practice public courtesy, we would stay away from attacking strangers for behaving in ways we don't approve of, out there in public.

A person might be aware of his or her mistake, or momentary indiscretion, or might even be deliberately indiscrete at the moment because of inner frustration rooted in anger or rage.

We do everyone a favor when we leave the person alone to sort out the problem—unless they are putting others at risk.

If we can't intervene to help, we should desist from interfering lest we harm, if the person's behavior or conduct is doing harm to no one.

However, if the person's behavior is creating an inconvenience for us, self-respect would demand that we do not behave belligerently, or even angrily, especially when the person is a total stranger. A very firm courteous approach, without sarcasm, is more likely to be effective than a belligerently confrontational stance.

When the way we say what we think we must say, is full of understanding, compassion, and respect, we appeal to the good in others. Likewise, when we share good feelings we lessen the risk of violent responses. Empathy and compassion tend to dissolve hostility.

Please excuse the language used in the following story, and perhaps in a few others. It is by no means the language I use, because I come with goodwill and pure love for all. But when we are not feeling good about ourselves we are sometimes full of anger, and that anger is sometimes left to ferment and build up so much noxious energy within us, till, like a stink bomb, it implodes within us, poisoning every form of communication emanating from us.

So I will give you the language of ill will and anger so that those still using it would recognize where it could lead. And then I will give the language of good will and compassion, so those who did not know about this more acceptable language could come to embrace it, and perhaps by so doing, spread goodwill, and perhaps even extend the years of their lives.

# STORY #2

# Lucky Yuh Didn't Hit My Car

◆ ◆ ◆

One man is out driving. It is a lovely sunny afternoon. His seven year old daughter, and five year old son, with their eight year old girl cousin are in the back seat, smacking their lips on some tasty popsicles.

Another driver, a security guard, returning home from a twelve-hour shift, perhaps in a brief moment of misjudgment, mind wandering, or drowsiness—who knows—almost collides with the father's vehicle. But he swerves away in time and avoids an accident.

The father, also pulls sharply away from what for a split second seemed to be a sure smash up. In the commotion, the popsicles fall to the floor, forgotten, as the children scream hysterically. The security guard unaware of the ruckus in the other vehicle, is driving ahead of the man with the children in his car. He imagines the father is angry at him but he is thankful a collision was miraculously avoided.

Shocked and shaken by the raging, bellowing voice screaming from the vehicle speeding up alongside his vehicle, the security guard slows down and is confronted with the scowling face of the driver, even as he hears the terrified screams of the children, and the racial slurs of the father screaming, "Yuh blankety blank ignorant fool! Yuh lucky yuh didn't hit my car here today!"

And the eight year old girl cousin, with anger  in her tone, screams at the man, "Yuh stupid, or what?"

The two younger children, looking confused and scared, locate their popsicles.

By this time the father pulls in front the man's car, gets out his vehicle in a rage, and gesticulating, storms over to the other car, which at this time, is prevented from moving. He is gesticulating and behaving belligerently, like he's determined to attack the security guard in his car.

The alarmed security guard eases out of his car and backs away. He tries to apologize, but the father is too besides himself with rage to hear apologies. With a volley of expletives rolling off his tongue, he lunges at the security guard.

The children are terrified. Even the eight year old is now crouching down in her seat They all want to go home. The seven-year-old and five-year-old wish their father would just get back in his car and take them home.

In no time the two men are up in each other's face, both shouting, but neither listening.

And expletives are flying right and left.

Crouching in fear, the children remain still, very still. All they want is for the driver of the other car to drive off and their father to return to his place behind the steering wheel and take them home.

From somewhere nearby they hear a soft snapping sound. It sounded like a firecracker. They wait. They listen. No more angry voices. They step out of the car and look around.

No one is setting off fireworks.

They are not seeing their dad. They walk around the vehicle. Their dad is lying on the ground. Their popsicles fall from their hands. The seven and five year old shake their father.

"Daddy! Daddy, get up", they cry.

"Uncle! Uncle, wake up", the eight year old sobs.

But the father does not move. And he does not answer.

Away from the other car, in a bushy area, off the road,  the other driver is holding the phone to his ear, with one hand, and massaging the back of his neck, with the other hand. He looks worried.

Vehicles are stopping. A crowd is gathering.

The District Medical Officer has to be called to give permission to remove the body to the morgue.

It would be hours before the children return home to a life that would be forever different.

In a moment, it seems, the security guard on his way home after a long shift, becomes a murderer. And the father taking his children and niece for a pleasant afternoon drive, becomes a corpse.

Everyone's life is forever changed.

But it didn't have to end so; it could have ended differently.

## *Story #2. Ending Differently*

The driver almost ran into the car with the children in the back seat, but swerves away in time.

"Sorry man," he shouts, pulling abreast of the vehicle.

The father gives an understanding wave, and slows down. He pulls aside, signaling the other driver to pull aside, on the not too busy back road.

"That was close," the father calls out. "Are you all right?"

"Sorry. I must have dozed off. I didn't realize I was so sleepy. I'm now returning home from a twelve-hour shift."

"God must have been watching over us today, boy. You think you could get home safely?"

"Yes. But I need to stop off by some family who live in the area, and take a rest. Later on I'll go home. I don't want to risk falling asleep behind the wheel again. I might not be this lucky next time."

"That's the best thing, man. When sleep ready to take over, boy, sometimes it doesn't give us any warning."

"Glad you understand."

"Man, it can happen to the best of us."

Despite this warm interchange the father recognizes in himself, a bit of anger. He searches himself and recognizes that he has some unkind feelings to people of racial groups other than his own. But what is his own? He is mixed—very mixed.

He knows he felt good talking to this particular man, but he remembered the first wave of negative feelings that washed over him when he first glimpsed the man who almost collided with his vehicle.

What was that fleeting negative feeling about? Was that latent hostility towards his grandmother's family?

He will go and have a talk with a counselor, and talk about those feelings of anger that disturb him when he thinks of certain ethnic and racial groups.

He thinks of the children there on the back seat, enjoying their popsicles. The world would be safer if they and their generation would accept and respect all peoples, and not devise any excuse for disrespecting any person.

It seems that in no time the father is back home.

His wife greets him fondly. She's unaware of how close he came to putting an end to their relationship, forever.

The children wash their sticky hands and lips, and say a happy goodbye to their cousin. They would all remember fondly the very pleasant conversation their father had with the driver of the vehicle that almost drove them off the road.

Everyone goes on with life as usual.

The DMO has a beautiful, undisturbed evening. And the security guard goes his way merrily, happy that he had such a pleasant encounter with such an agreeable fellow road user.

# STORY #3

# Arrogant Doctor

◆ ◆ ◆

The father is worried about his son's vision. He had taken the boy to several General Practitioners. All of them said the same thing—the boy needed to be examined by an eye specialist. The father carries the boy to an Optometrist.

The Optometrist closely examines the boy's eyes. He tells the worried father that the boy needs to be seen by a medical doctor, an ophthalmologist. He suggests also that the father get more than one opinion.

Worried that his son might have contracted some serious eye disease, or might have developed some dangerous eye condition, the father carries his son to three different ophthalmologists. He desperately hopes the grim news they all gave him would go away.

If he could find one, just one doctor, to dispute the diagnosis of all these other doctors with their message of gloom for his boy . . . if only. He had to pray and hope.

The family had been doing without some household necessities to afford the medical bills, but he was willing to make the sacrifice.

Everybody he spoke to about his son's condition suggested that he carry the boy to a well-known, long serving eye doctor located in the heart of town.

The father had never before had any cause to search out eye specialists so he had never even heard of this older man, a well-respected eye specialist.

Father and son are in the examination room. The elderly doctor peers intently into the boy's eyes.

The father is very anxious.

Would this doctor's findings be different from the findings of the other doctors'?

He prays that this doctor would tell him that whatever is happening to his boy's eyes can be handled, that *the problem can be licked.*

All he needs is a little hope that his boy is not really in any danger of losing his sight.

Unable to contain his anxiety any longer, the father decides to share his burden with the elderly doctor. He would tell him why he really brought his boy for the eye examination.

"Doctor, I had carried my son to three other specialists before I brought him here. I am so worried; I just want to get the best professional advice. I just want to know that there is still a chance that my boy's sight can be saved."

Without a word, the doctor straightens up stiffly. He drops his hands, and then hastily puts away the equipment he was using on the boy.

"Get out of my office," he snaps, staring at the man icily.

"What did you say?"

The totally befuddled father cannot believe that this is really happening.

"Get out of my office. And pay my secretary the full fee."

"But you are not through with the examination. You haven't given me any results."

The elderly man marches off icily. The confused father, hurting for his and his son's wounded pride, and more distressed now about his son's ailment, pays the secretary, and leaves. He is full of anger, full of pain, and full of confused feelings about what he should do next.

Over the next couple weeks, the father would relate this incident to family, friends, and professionals—to any who would listen. He talks to release his feelings of bewilderment. But no amount of talking seems to remove the gut wrenching pain and embarrassment he feels for himself and his son.

"No medical person should treat members of the public like that", he says. My son and I did not deserve that disrespect. The doctor should not have charged us for service that was not given. Am I wrong to seek different medical opinions? I thought the medical people were here to help us.

"This elderly doctor came highly recommended. I can't understand this doctor's attitude. All I wanted was help for my child. If I was a different kind of man, I would look for some way to get even with that doctor.

"I can't believe that man ordered me and my son out of his office, when he was in the midst of attending to my child. And he ordered me out just because I told him I had gone to him for another opinion. I am just so angry. I am going to the newspapers and to all the talk shows and tell the world about this man who everybody thinks is such an honorable professional! The people should be warned!"

This encounter could have ended differently It didn't have to end so!

## Story # 3. Ending Differently

◆ ◆ ◆

The doctor is peering intently into the boy's eyes.

"Doctor, I carried my son to three other ophthalmologists before coming to you. I just want to get the best professional opinion about my boy's condition."

"Oh?"

"Yes. I've been so worried. I just want to be sure that there is some agreement at least among three or four eye doctors."

"Well, I think I could understand that. You would want to be sure we know what the problem is. At least two of us should agree."

"Two?"

"I should think so."

"Okay."

"I must confess though, when I heard you say that before coming to me you had carried your son to three other doctors, I felt a bit alarmed. I wondered if you were questioning my professional competency."

"Not at all, doctor. It's neither about you nor your colleagues.

It's my son's vision I am concerned about. I just want the best for him. Maybe at least two of you could talk, you know, consult together."

"That could be arranged."

And the father leaves the ophthalmologist's office, with renewed confidence in the medical profession, and feeling hopeful about his son's vision.

# Note 1

*One's life can be threatened by a physical weapon, which in a moment, just like that, could be used to sever the vital link. But one's life could also be snipped away little by little by one stressful encounter after another.*

*One never knows which snip would accomplish the final severance, which proverbial straw would break the camel's back.*

*When the public goes to health professionals usually they are already stressed. They go for ease, not for exacerbation of their stress.*

*Health professionals, perhaps more than many other service providers, can, by treating the people with sensitivity and respect, help to relieve much of their stress.*

# STORY #4

# Cruel Secret

◆ ◆ ◆

He had met her during the course of his work and she seemed to be such a sweet person, so friendly and helpful, he decided to see her again.

He called and she called. Soon they had a strong friendship going. But she was becoming very possessive. She wanted to always know where he was and everything he did when he was away from her.

She was so persistent, if she did not reach him, she would call his parents' home at any hour of the day or night to enquire about his whereabouts.

He knew he had to end the relationship. He could not let someone he had come to know for just six months take over his entire life like this!

Even if he had known her for a couple years, he would not tolerate her trying to swallow him up into her own life, like she evidently was attempting to do.

He told her he could not cope with her possessiveness, so they had to stop seeing each other.

She became very angry, and went into a depression. When that didn't work, she called him and threatened to kill herself if he left her.

He did not want to carry that guilt throughout his life. But he was not going to allow himself to be manipulated by this woman or by anybody else.

"This relationship is not going anywhere", he said to her. "We have to end. I'm finished. I won't be seeing you again."

"I know you have somebody else", she retorted.

"It's not about anybody else," he defended himself. "I am miserable in this relationship. We are just two completely different types of people."

"So? Being different is not bad. We could always be learning from each other. You just don't want to give account."

"Look, I have made up my mind. I value my freedom. I can't have anybody trying to make me account for every moment of my life. I don't belong to you. I belong to myself. If you can't trust me that is your problem. Just leave me alone. I don't understand why you would want to be with me anyway when we are always quarreling. And stop calling my parents' home. You disturb them all hours of the night. You are intruding on their privacy. They are not accustomed to this kind of invasion of their privacy. Have respect for my parents' right to be free of your harassment."

"I don't harass your parents. I call them only when I can't get on to you."

"Just leave them alone, and stop calling their phone."

"I might as well be dead," she lashed out. "If you leave me, I'm going to kill myself. I have already cut my wrist with a razor blade. And I know just how I'm going to finish the job. Just remember, if I kill myself it would be your fault."

"I don't want you to kill yourself. But if you make an attempt on your life, how could that be my fault?"

"Because you reneged on your promise."

"What promise?"

"You said you would never leave me. That was what you said right after we made love the last time. After we have been together for so long, I don't think I could go on without you."

"Ha, nice try. That promise was made in the heat of passion. You can make out very well without me. You have so much going for you, why would you want to hold on to me anyway?"

"Because I love you, and you swore you'd never leave me."

"But we don't get along. You said you were in love with the boyfriend you had before me."

"Yes, I was."

"Maybe you still are."

"Maybe."

"And it could be that you are holding on to me because you are confusing me with him. You ever thought of that?"

"No."

"Why don't you give him a call? He might be glad to take you back. You said you two were so close."

"Yes, we were close. But we can't get back together."

"Why not? He is married?"

"He is dead."

"What did you say?"

"I said, he is dead."

"That was what I thought I heard you say. How long ago?"

"About eight months ago."

"Why didn't you tell me?"

"Because you would have left me."

"Why would I leave you because your former boyfriend . . . is . . . dead? Wait . . . a . . . minute. What did he die from?"

"Why are you asking me?"

"I'm asking because I need to know."

"You've figured it out already."

"You're joking, aren't you? Tell me you're joking! Woman, tell me you are joking!"

"Stop screaming in my ears. Do I sound like somebody who is joking?"

"Oh my God! What kind of woman are you? Why didn't you tell me?"

"Tell you what, that my boyfriend died of AIDS? Nobody dies from AIDS, anyhow. Cause of death was pneumonia."

# Note 2

*Obviously, this story did not have to end so! It could have ended differently.*

## Story #4. Ending Differently

He had met her during the course of his work and was very attracted to her. He called, and she called.

"Let's get to know each other better," he says.

"What do you have in mind?" she asks.

"We could go out together with some of my friends sometimes."

"Friends? Why friends?"

"These are the people I hang out with. A couple of them are married, and we all hang out together at times. If you don't want to go with my friends, it's okay. I'm open for suggestions."

"What about going to your place?" she asks.

"I don't have my own place. I still live with my parents. I will have to ask them if you can come over. Maybe my mom would invite you to dinner."

"Forget it. I thought I was talking with a man. I could see you are still a boy. You have to ask Mama!"

"What's wrong with respecting my mother? I don't have any question about my manhood. I just respect my parents' home."

"What could we do with your Mama around?"

"Are you saying you want to have sex?"

"Why not? Isn't that what people do when they are getting to know each other?"

"I thought people try to become friends when they're getting to know each other. There's lots of time for sex after marriage."

"Ha-ha. You are joking, aren't you?"

"I have decided not to arouse anybody sexually unless I'm married to them."

"Where have you come from? Nobody talks like that out here."

"I do. And considering what's happening today, I know I have made the right decision."

"So what? You're telling me you never had sex?"

"I'm saying what my decision is. I had to come up with some standards for myself. I'm not saying I was always like this. But how am I going to live with integrity if I don't have some standards for myself? I had to make up some rules to help me live the kind of life I always wanted to have."

"You sound like you're still holding on to childhood ideals. I used to think like that, but I have seen the real world. All that fairy book kind of life doesn't exist for anybody in the real world."

"Life is what we make it."

"Where you come from? Life is hell. Life is nothing but hell. Who cares about values and integrity? You go out there trying to be the perfect gentleman, and watch how you'll find yourself being kicked around. This life is about taking what you can get, however you can get it, and enjoying it for as long as you can enjoy it. Your prudish kinds of standards don't work out here in the real world. You belong to one of those Christian churches? That's where all this talk is coming from?"

"I attend a church, yes. Don't you?"

"I can't tell the last time I was in a church, except . . . for a funeral . . . I know some guys who go to church, but they're not like you. Some of them won't go all the way with the girl, but I don't see any difference between what they do, and sex. The only thing they don't do, is enter. To me, them so fooling themselves and playing games."

"I have decided to wait till I am married to get involved in sexual intercourse. And to me, foreplay is part of that whole scene, so until I'm married, I'm not going back there."

"So what if the girl is willing to settle for foreplay alone?"

"If that is where a girl's mind and interest is, she is not the girl for me. For me, it is not how far I could go without crossing the line. It is about getting to know each other. I would rather be attracted to a girl's mind than to her body. Her mind is what I would have to live with. Any male and female can engage in sex. Not every mind will hold my interest.  I would have to feel very comfortable with a girl's mind before I could even start feeling interested in her sexually."

"You are different."

"I suppose everyone has to define their values for themselves."

"I suppose so."

"What about you? What rules do you live by?"

"I never thought of that before. But I realize something about myself, now that you are asking."

"Yes? What's that?"

"I think I have a rule somewhere deep in my head that says, 'don't do anything that would make them reject you'."

"That's interesting. How far would you go to make sure you're not rejected?"

"You wouldn't want to know."

"But you might anticipate rejection where there might be none. And you could end up paying a price you didn't really have to pay, just to be accepted."

"Granted. I will still do what I think I have to do to protect myself from rejection from a man, though. If a man says he likes me, and he wants me, I give myself to him. I would think of consequences afterwards."

"You sell yourself cheap."

"Hey, I'm not exactly choice merchandise. I take what I'm offered."

"What a pity. You always have a choice. You're selling yourself cheap. And you don't have to."

"What kind of girl you think you would look for when you are ready to make a commitment?"

"Definitely a woman who is about developing her mind, and trying to make the world a better place for all of us."

"That's it?"

"Well, I have some other items on my wish list, but these are the ones I won't compromise on."

"So what if she has physical needs before marriage?"

"You mean if she would want us to be sexually involved before marriage?"

"Yes."

"I don't see myself even getting interested in a girl who is so heavily interested in sex, she would want to rush me. I am not saying it is not possible. But if I love her and she is hot on sex, I'll have to help her learn to wait."

"Ha, you don't know what it feels like to want to be with somebody, and there is nobody to be with, you know. Your whole body feels like it's going crazy, you know. It's like all other parts of your brain shut down, and all you have is this craving."

"Ever heard of sublimation, channeling the energy into some other useful activity?"

"No, but then I wouldn't be interested."

"There are too many other things for me to fill my life with right now. And you know what? I'm not ashamed of my decision to stay away from sexual encounters. I don't think you should be ashamed of waiting till marriage either. You would feel better about yourself when you wait to share your body with your marriage partner. Even if you have been promiscuous up till now, you could decide to go celibate. In today's world, it is safe to wait."

"Great lecture, but too late for me, virgin boy. Where have you come from, anyway? Nobody talks like that these days."

"That's not true. I do."

"My boyfriend would have laughed in your face."

"That's okay. I don't need anybody's approval to stand by my decision. So why isn't he here making you happy, anyway? If you love him so much, why are you coming after me?"

"He's not here because we reached the end of our road together. He was great in bed, though. And unlike you he didn't care if his parents were at home or not at home. I practically lived in his room."

"Different values. Why two people would want to be always in a closed bedroom, is more than I can understand. How much sex do you need anyway when it is leading to nowhere? Do you see married people always in a bedroom? There is so much more to life than sex."

"I like the thrills. I live for the thrills."

"And after the thrills, what? Where do thrills take you?"

"I don't bother with all those questions. My father was successful, and he didn't ask all those questions when he was having sex with me more times than I can count."

"Incest?"

"Yes. I've been having sex since I was small."

"Well, you more than many other persons should understand that sex isn't all that there is to friendship. How you feel about your father now?"

"Whenever I think of him getting into me I feel like vomiting till all my insides turn inside out. I wish I could scrub his nastiness out of me."

"Where is he now?"

"Dead. That drunk! That pathetic, powerful, rich, evil, diabolical drunk that was my father! That pervert used to have his friends come over to have sex with me."

"And where was your mother?"

"With him. Hand in glove. They were evil."

"Where is your mother now?"

"Where she belongs—with him."

"I'm sorry. You've had it hard."

"Hard is all I know. So, if I remember, all this talk started because you wanted us to go out together some place. But definitely not with your friends.

"Where do you want us to go?"

"Actually, I really don't want to take you anywhere. I think we have just gotten to know each other quite well."

"That's it? You don't want us to be friends?"

"We could be friends, casual friends, with no obligations, and definitely no dating."

"What happen, I'm too much for you?"

"Let's say, we are about different things."

"Fair enough."

"So, where is your boyfriend now?"

"Dead."

"Dead?"

"Yep."

"How long ago?"

"About eight months."

"He was sick?"

"Yes."

"What did he die from? How come you're not answering? Was it AIDS?"

"He died from pneumonia. Nobody dies from AIDS."

"But he had AIDS?"

"Yes."

"Oh my God. And you would have allowed me to have sex with you, and you would not have told me . . .?"

"I told you I would do anything to safeguard myself against rejection from any man."

"Are you angry at him?"

"Why should I be? He should be angry at me."

# Note 3

*Notice how we changed the outcome here? We communicate not only by words, but also by behavior. But preceding all behavior are the thoughts, our thoughts.*

*The young man was alert. He was thinking, and listening, and weighing what he was hearing. And he was hearing a lot through the young woman's behavior.*

*Because he was alert he avoided entangling his life in frustration and false guilt. He had embraced some moral values that gave character to his life, and saved him from rushing into a relationship with a woman who felt so desperately in need of sexual satisfaction she was willing to endanger his life to get what she wanted.*

*Now he does not have to worry about feeling manipulated by a woman who would use threat of suicide to keep him where she could use him. He stayed on the safe side. He did not cross the line. Adherence to principles of morality saved and empowered him.*

# STORY #5

# Forced Into Marriage

◆ ◆ ◆

The father cautioned his young adult daughter, "That boy does not belong to our religion; he is not one of us. I don't want you to have anything to do with him. We will get a nice boy from among our people for you."

"But I love my boyfriend, Papa."

"Shut your mouth and have some respect. I said you are not to see that boy. I don't want him coming 'round your job. I don't want to hear that you are even seen with him."

The young adult daughter runs away from home. She is a responsible girl, so she finds shelter with a very responsible family.

Meanwhile she fears that her father might not stop searching till he finds her. And he does search till he finds her. He is angry as he confronts his daughter in her temporary home.

She is twenty-seven, and working at a responsible job. She takes care of herself financially. He no longer has any economic responsibility for her, yet he feels responsible for this daughter of his. This is his child. He and his wife spent almost their entire married life taking good care of her.

She is a lovely girl. He would not allow her to make a bad choice at this stage of her life. He and his wife did not take their time bringing her up carefully for her to now throw everything away behind some man she fancies she is in love with.

The man she imagined herself in love with, didn't have a thing to offer her. What kind of life would his child have with that man?

Until she could think straight, he will take control of her. And if she thinks she is so much of a woman she could do what she wants, he would break her hands, and keep her at home till the bones mend. Maybe by then she would get some sense in her head.

The father orders the daughter to pack her things and leave the house with him. He threatens to break some part of her body with the piece of wood he is holding if she refuses to return home and marry the man he and her mother had chosen for her.

He threatens her in the presence of her host family.

To spare her benefactors further embarrassment, she goes with her father. Within a few weeks the wedding is arranged, and within a few months she is married to the boy chosen by her parents.

She is more than ever in love with her former boyfriend, and feels only contempt for the lovely man she has been forced to call husband. They are all miserably unhappy, even her father.

But it didn't have to end so.

## Story #5. Ending Differently

◆ ◆ ◆

"Daughter, I am feeling very disturbed. I see you with a certain young man, but he does not belong to our religion. And you know that we don't allow our children to marry anyone who does not belong to our religion. Besides, he is not one of our people."

"But Papa, I love him. I don't want to marry that man you and Mama want me to marry. I hate that man. The sight of him *makes my blood crawl.*"

"I did not know you disliked this man so much. Daughter, he is a good man. He belongs to a good family. This is the right man for you."

"Papa, only God knows who is right for me."

"You are right, Daughter. But I know who is wrong for you. I don't want to see you unhappy. But understand our situation. We are responsible for the type of families our children set up. It is our duty to see you married to someone who will honor you and bring honor to our family. And it is our duty to prevent you from marrying anyone outside our religion, and not of our culture—anyone we think won't be able to provide well for you. You are a lovely girl. You deserve the best. I'm not going to allow you to choose what is not best for you."

"But Father, my boyfriend is from our culture. He belongs to our race."

"Daughter, he might look like us, but people from that religion have a completely different lifestyle. Your life with that man would be hell. I am not going to allow you to throw away all chance for happiness by marrying anybody like that."

"I don't know what to do, Papa. But I'd rather die than marry this man you want me to marry. I think I will die if you force him on me."

"Then would you promise to break off the friendship with that man if we promise not to force you to marry this man?"

"Yes, Papa. I would do just about anything to get out of having to marry this man. But it wouldn't be easy. I truly love my boyfriend. I don't know if I would ever love anybody else."

"Sometimes in life we have to release that which is not for us, even if in releasing it we suffer great agony. You will be stronger after the suffering. And maybe after some time you would even see more clearly. As long as we understand one thing—you cannot marry outside our religious culture."

# Note 4

*The above outcome is a very conservative one, and might be uncommon today. Many parents today are not that adamant about preventing their son or daughter from marrying outside their culture, though they may show their displeasure in other ways.*

# STORY #6

# Taking Threat Seriously

Another woman had a child for her husband.

She had been the self-sacrificing wife, scrimping here, pinching there, to make sure they could get what they needed in the house. He was the only one bringing in a salary so she took care of all his needs and all the children's needs.

By not asking for that slipper, or new dress, or hat for church, she thought she was being reasonable. But now he was buying milk and diapers for his child and groceries for the woman. In addition, he was giving the woman a monthly allowance.

She felt cheated—thought she would go mad. To quiet her down, he told her that he was not seeing the woman anymore. Still she was always seeing evidence that he was a regular visitor to the woman's house.

◆ ◆ ◆

He loved his newborn. And in his own way, loved his wife. He didn't like the quarreling, and bad attitude she was showing just because he had this child. What could he do? This was his child. He had to be with his child as much as he could.

The children he had with his wife were bigger. They were always *up under their mother*. They weren't acting as though they cared about him much anymore, anyhow. Whenever he entered the house everybody would be silent. Nobody would have anything much to do with him.

But over here by the child's mother he felt appreciated. At least he didn't have to look at the sour face of his wife, when he was there, and he didn't have to feel stares of contempt directed at him.

He wished he could stay by the woman more, just to be with his child. But he didn't want to jeopardize his marriage. He and his wife had built a very comfortable home together. And his wife was an organized woman.

What they had was dignity. Their home felt organized and solid. His wife had made their home a family. Furthermore, he was already over forty-five. He didn't want to go trying to set up house with this young woman he had the child with, although that was what she wanted, and what her mother wanted.

He thought long and hard about his marriage, as he drove along the city streets, making his way to the child's mother's house on the outskirts of the city. He was married to a good, god-fearing, praying woman. He knew that. She was too chaste to ever think of cheating on him.

He could trust her.

He wondered about all the expectations his wife seemed to have of him. What did she expect?

He wasn't a perfect man, and he wished she would stop behaving as though he had a right to be perfect just because she wanted a perfect husband.

He wished his wife would just quiet herself and stop acting as though their marriage had come to an end just because he had a child out there.

It wasn't as though he had stopped supporting his home. He was a man, not some little church boy. Why couldn't he have an outside woman?

He thought of all his partners who had their outside woman. Only now and then he ever heard of a wife *giving her husband horrors.*

Most of the men had their wives under control.

His wife was in turmoil. She had never ever in her wildest imagination, thought she would ever have to put up with sharing her husband with another woman.

And look who he went and chose, a woman with all her youthful vigor.

She felt used, old even, when compared to that woman. She had spent away her youth looking after him, the house, and the children. And now he had abandoned her for this young girl.

They always had their moments of chilliness. But she felt she could cope with just any kind of problem as long as he respected the integrity of their marriage.

Now, however, she was living through her worst nightmare. She felt disrespected, dumped, humiliated, yet compelled to hold her head up.

She had to take care of her precious children. They were suffering too, because he had stopped spending time with them.

For a long time, he had been so rough with them, the children had become afraid of him.

It was bad enough getting news about him and the woman, but she felt as though he had plunged a knife into her heart when she saw him that day with the woman and child in the front seat of his car.

"What my wife expects me to do?", he asked himself after the blow out with her. "I have a child with the woman. I must take her out. If she needs anything, I must take her to get it."

"My God, the man has lost all respect for me", the wife sighed to herself. "When I asked him why he was seen with the woman, he snapped at me 'and *ah* have *ah* child with she; *ah* muss be seen with she sometimes'. No respect whatsoever! No compassion."

Despite all her sacrifices, and attempts to be accommodating to him, under these difficult circumstances, she felt she was not getting any respect, any consideration, from him.

He ignored her personal need for intimacy and reassurance, when he felt like ignoring her. And he demanded that she yield her body to him when he felt like having her.

It seemed that he had lost all consideration for her feelings. It hadn't been always like this.

She was so distressed, she thought her head would split. She needed someone to talk with, somebody who could show a little compassion, some kind of understanding.

There was no way she would even think of talking to her young children about her distress. She knew some mothers who burdened their children's minds with their heavy personal adult problems, but she felt she could not do that to her children. She could not confuse them. She must allow them to become adults gradually.

And she definitely could not talk with him.

Her body felt tight with tension. She felt she would go off if she didn't find someone to talk to. Somewhere there had to be somebody she could talk with.

She became convinced that thought creates reality when soon after saying to herself that she had to find someone to talk with, she ran into an old high school friend. He had been away for many years, and was resettling in the country.

This could not be happening by chance, she thought, as conversation flowed. She had found someone who knew how to listen. This was so relieving to her.

The friend listened caringly. And so a friendship grew with this friend, an unmarried man, a few years younger than she.

It was a friendship, not an affair.

Her husband had laid a violent hand on her once before. It had taken her years to get over that. He had never been physically violent since that time.

Now he wanted to know the identity of the man calling his house for his wife. She told him about the chance meeting with her old school friend. She had nothing to hide.

But then the calls kept on coming. He couldn't believe she was talking to another man, regularly. He asked her what was going on, and she said nothing was going on. Then he ordered her to tell the man to stop calling his house.

The calls stopped. But some weeks later the woman got word that the man had been due to leave the country. Alarmed that he was leaving, she called him on her cell phone. He returned her call.

Unknown to her, her husband had checked her cell phone that evening.

"You still in touch with that man?" His voice was hostile.

"Sometimes."

"But you know I don't want you talking to him."

"The man is just a friend. I don't know what you getting on about?"

"Hah, you don't know who you playing with, you know. I could kill, you know."

"Kill who?"

"Kill you, woman. You don't know how furious I feeling right now, you know."

"You better check yourself, boy. That fury is not about me. If I was doing like you, what you would say? Where all this rage coming from? Check yourself, boy. I am not your problem."

When the children had been tucked into bed for the night, he wordlessly cornered her and held her by the throat as he pummeled her.

She was in shock, terrified for her life, and had to assume in the midst of her terror that somehow he had found out about her communication with the man that day.

He had attacked her like this once before. She did not want to frighten the children, so she tried to take the blows without bawling out, even as she struggled to free her throat from his powerful grip.

When he threw her on the floor and started pressing his knees into her stomach while choking her, she knew he intended to kill her. Several years earlier he had attacked her like this.

This man had sworn to protect and serve. He knew just how and where, to inflict the blows and put the pressure, to make her scared for her life.

Her gasping cries awoke the children, and the husband who wanted *to save face* with the children, let her alone for the rest of the night.

This couldn't be happening to her, she thought. How dare this man cross the line! She did not know what she would do.

She wept, enraged.

It was killing her to think that he still insisted on being intimate with her whenever he chose. She felt so denigrated, so humiliated. All she could do was lie still like a log, and wonder how she could get him to use a condom every time he used her.

But the indignity was too much.

An idea came to her. She will take care of him while he slept.

Deep in sleep, he felt a flat metallic blow against his thigh. Eyes flying open, he braced himself to sit up, but quietly eased back down.

She wasn't a feather-weight woman.

Holding the shining blade, ready to swipe, she warned him, "Put your hand on me one more time, and you would never again sleep comfortably in this house. . .. Yes, I am a church going woman, but I'll be damned if I allow the likes of you to humiliate and terrorize me one more time. Boy, either you kill me, or I kill you.

"You out there living a nasty life, and dare to attack me. Why you think you have the right to put your nasty hands on me for talking with a friend when you out there making all kinds of little girls pregnant?

"Boy, you put your filthy hands on me once before, and I didn't hit back; but there isn't going to be a third time. *Allyuh* men think *allyuh* could control your outside women, and your wife too. You play me for a fool long enough. I done playing, boy. I done.

"Furthermore, stay out of my bed, and don't ever try to be intimate with me again."

That was virtually the end of their marriage.

But it didn't have to end so.

# Note 5

*A marriage relationship is so intricate in its dynamics, telling even a detailed story of any part of it could never give a true reflection of all the subterranean forces at play in even one interaction. But we have to start somewhere. So let's see how I could guide the communication between these two people to bring some measure of understanding, and so prevent yet another tragedy.*

*Or even let's see how I can save a wandering, self-loathing, frustrated and abusive husband from becoming an unsuspecting victim of revenge.*

*Mind you, any deep change in communication would have to be preceded by much introspection, repentance, surrender, and commitment.*

*All of this is inner work—work between an individual and that supremely greater power known as their higher self.*

*However, this couple is in crisis mode. Either of them could kill the other or be killed by the other right now. I have to keep them safe. So let's see how we could have this story ending, perhaps not perfectly, but for now, differently.*

## *Story #6. Ending Differently*

She heard he had a child, and felt she would go mad. This wasn't just a passing affair.

A child stays in the relationship and in your life, forever.

All her scrimping and saving to make ends meet was now going to benefit that woman and his child.

She confronts him.

"This is your child. I have not been sacrificing all these years so another woman could benefit."

"What do you want me to do?"

"I need to have five hundred dollars more each month."

"I give the child's mother four hundred dollars a month. I won't have any money for myself if I give you five hundred more every month."

"That is your problem. You chose to go out of the marriage and have a child."

"You think I planned to have this child. I didn't go looking for a child."

"You're a grown man. When a man is unfaithful and goes and

has sex with a woman other than his wife, he runs the risk of getting the woman pregnant.

You chose to have sex with the woman. You are responsible for getting her pregnant. You went after your fun; you pay the consequences. I am not staying without things I need anymore, so you could support another woman."

# Note 6

*I'm not saying that all of the above is the ideal kind of interaction that should proceed in a case like this, but we are dealing with two real human beings here. The woman is hurt, so she is not going to suddenly become angelic and unconditional in her loving because she is learning to talk it out rather than pull out her hair and pelt him down with every utensil she could find in the kitchen. The important thing here is that they are talking about the problem, and this of itself is healthy.*

"What you want me to do? I would have to find some other way to earn, maybe get a second job for the time being."

"Well do it."

"That wouldn't leave me much free time for myself. I wouldn't be able to see the children much."

"You hardly spend time with the children anyhow. That's how you come to have this child in the first place. You had too much free time. And none of it was spent with our children. You were too busy doing whatever makes a woman pregnant. You still don't spend time with our family."

"Well, I have to work, you know."

"I thought you were at work yesterday, but I was driving through town in a taxi when I saw your car."

"I went to see the child, and the child's mother wanted to get something in town, so I carried her. This is not going to be easy, you know. I have to see my child. And my child lives with the mother, and the woman would need to get some things in town sometimes. I don't know how we will work this out."

"I don't know either. I thought the front seat of that car was mine. I see now it belongs to your child's mother too."

"I don't know what to say to you, *nah*."

"It was going after her that caused you to have the child. Now going to see the child could lead you right back to her. So how many children you would have with this woman before this is over?"

"You must be know what you talking about."

"I don't think I could stay in this marriage. I don't want to be one of these women who represent one of a man's multiple families. I really can't take this."

"So what you going to do?"

"We need to talk with a counselor. All I know is that this trouble you have brought on our home is driving me crazy."

"A big man like me going to sit down and tell my business to some woman, or man. I'm not a little child to have anybody tell me what to do."

"I need to have somebody help me decide what to do, because I definitely can't live the rest of my life like this. I feel scandalized—humiliated. That young woman is your woman. And I am sharing sex with a man who is sharing sex with that woman? The thought of it makes me sick."

"The woman and I done. I've told you that over and over."

"Your word means nothing to me. You have lied and lied all through the past two years you've been with that woman. We go to a counselor or this marriage won't be a true marriage ever again."

Some time has elapsed, and the husband has become aware that his wife has a friend.

"Who is that man I saw you talking to in town today?"

"A friend from way back. He was away, and came back recently."

"He looked like more than a friend, to me. How come you all were eating together at the hamburger shop? You had a date?"

"The man is a friend. He knew I was waiting on you and we sat in the restaurant talking, till you showed up. Nobody was eating."

"That is the same one you call sometimes?"

"Yes. We are friends. We talk. God knows I need to have somebody to talk with around here."

"Let us make a truce. I won't go out with the child's mother, and you don't arrange to meet this man."

"A A. But I never arranged to meet the man. I tell you we met by chance in town. What you want me to do if I see him, turn my back on him? I can't do that. The man has been my friend for years."

"I want you to stop calling him. And tell him to stop calling you."

"What trouble is this, Lord? Okay. But I can't stop him from calling me. I could only promise not to call him."

"You could tell him not to call you."

"You still talking to the man?"

"Yes. He calls sometimes."

"But I thought you promised not to have him call."

"Look, I can't let marriage become a prison for me, you know. I won't tolerate having you treat me as though I'm your child. I trust myself even if you don't trust me. It's belittling to have to deal with your suspiciousness."

"Woman, I ordered you not to call the man! I told you I don't want you talking to this man. You don't know how I'm feeling, you know. I am so angry, I could kill, you know. Ha, you don't know who you playing with, you know."

"Kill whom?"

"You!"

"You better examine that anger. I think you'd find it is directed against yourself. You're just projecting your disgust with yourself on to me."

"But you promised not to call the man, and not to have him call you."

"Look at yourself. Listen to yourself. You promised to cling to me only till death do us part. But God alone knows how many other women you must have been clinging to all these years. You got caught with one, and that's how I found out the kind of double life you have been living. God alone knows what diseases I must have picked up from your philandering. And you have the gall to pass judgment on me because I am talking with an old friend? And you're talking about killing? Boy, take a good look at yourself in the mirror."

"You think I'm joking. I'm telling you the truth, you know."

"Whenever anybody says they feel like killing, I believe they are telling the truth. I heard you, boy—loud and clear."

"Who you're calling?"

"My parents."

"So what you calling your parents for?"

"But what trouble is this? You don't want me to talk with somebody who is my friend, and now you are questioning my right to call my parents, my own parents?"

"What kind of double talk was that you all were carrying on with? You all have some kind of coded language?"

"Don't bother. They understood."

"That counselor thing—you really think a counselor could help?"

"They're always helping other people. I don't see why they can't help you."

"Me? I thought we were talking about our marriage."

"We can't do a thing about this marriage until you do something about yourself. You need to sort out whatever has you running around other women. And this anger in you that makes you feel like killing me for your own guilt, you need to get that sorted out also. If you feel like killing me for just talking with a friend, what would you want to do to me if I was like you, sleeping around with somebody out there? Look, somebody is at the door. You better see who it is."

"Goodnight sir. Someone called for the police."

"Police? I thought you were my in-laws. We didn't call for any police."

"I did."

"Why?"

"Officers, I want you to stay with me while I get my children and some things together. They don't know yet that we are moving out of here tonight. And Officers, I know my husband is one of your colleagues, but I hope you are here to protect me."

"We are, ma'am."

"Woman, what the hell you think you are doing? Look . . . I'll kill you . . . Officer, let me go! Let me go! I'll buss up this woman's mouth here tonight! I just here talking to the woman good, good, and she call the police for me like I am some common criminal!"

"Sir, we have to restrain you . . . fighting up with us will just make this harder for yourself . . . Quiet yourself . . . Look, your children are frightened. Quiet yourself. We will have to take you away. We have called for backup. Other officers are on their way. You will make it easier for all of us if you would quiet yourself."

"I'll kill this woman here tonight! I'll kill this woman!"

"Officer, you see for yourself what I am talking about?"

"Officers, O God, *allyuh* don't have to put handcuffs on me. Wait. Let me just go inside to get my wallet. Then I will go peacefully with *allyuh*."

"Officers, please keep my husband with you. I don't want to be like that woman who was murdered by her husband in the presence of the police when the husband tricked her and told her to come inside because he wanted to tell her something. Look, our daughter brought his wallet for him. I'm not going to let any man take my life from me foolishly."

"What's wrong with you, woman? Who talking about murder? Where you think you taking my children? One minute I talking to you, calm, calm, in the bedroom, next minute a set of police swarming in the house like I am some common criminal?"

"Boy, when you tell me you feel like killing me, I take you seriously, very seriously, boy. I *ent* making joke with my life, boy, nor with my children's lives. Don't forget I am the same woman you had on the floor of our bedroom with your knee on my chest and your hands around my throat."

"Woman, I didn't even remember that. That was years ago. I haven't laid a hand on you since!"

"And you won't ever again, not if I could help it. You can afford to forget, boy, but not me. I can't afford to forget that night you had your massive hands around my throat, and your knee pressing down on my chest. God alone knows how I didn't sustain broken ribs and a punctured lung. Boy, this is one woman who doesn't intend to wait around like a fool for a man to carry out his threat of murder. This is one woman who *ent* waiting 'round to be the next victim."

# STORY #7
# Get Out My Maxi!

◆ ◆ ◆

The middle-aged gentleman was glad to return to his country after about twenty years away. In time his name would be well known in the country, as one contributing to the enlightenment of the people. But as yet, he was little known.

Popular transportation was in the hands of private citizens whose minibuses were called maxis.

Recently returned home, after many years away, he was still to become fully acquainted with how the maxi doors worked.

Some maxi drivers would tell a passenger entering the vehicle, "Pull in the door, hard."

Other drivers would say, "Don't slam the door."

Some maxis had painted signs saying, "Don't slam".

Some had painted signs saying, "Close gently".

The gentleman had a lot on his mind. He was trying to get himself resettled in the country, and get his business started. This had been a long day for him. Without a vehicle to drive around, he had been doing lots of leg work in the hot, dry weather. He longed to get home, away from this huge, rush hour crowd of commuters waiting in the midst of the busy intersection, on transportation.

The maxi came, and he felt fortunate to get his foot in the door. He was the last one in. All the other seats had been taken. He found a seat just across from the door. Preparing to sit down, he pulled in the door behind him.

He was thankfully easing the weight off his feet, just behind the driver when the aged man swung his thick muscular neck around and snarled, "Get off my maxi!"

Stunned, to be confronted by the hawking roar and raging eyes glaring at him, the befuddled passenger was at a loss to know the cause of this sudden hostility.

"What?" the subdued gentleman asked, as the scowling driver seemed to strain to keep his head turned back.

"Get off my maxi!" the old man again roared, his eyes flaring disgust. "You slammed my door! Get off!"

And he looked as though he was ready to pull his stocky frame from behind the steering wheel and over the seat to help the passenger out with a powerful push, or even perhaps a kick.

"I'm sorry. I didn't mean to slam the door." The tired gentleman hoped the driver would cool down and leave him alone to get to his destination without further insults.

"Get off!" the stocky, bitter man bellowed.

Confused and upset, the man got off, to the joy of a woman who was being pushed by the crowd of commuters, to the maxi door.

His vehicle full of passengers, because every bit of aisle space

3

was fitted with a folding seat, the sour-faced driver drove off with his sourness and his bulging blood vessels which looked ready to pop.

And the energies in the ousted passenger bunched up in all kinds of emotional hurts for a while, beneath his outer composure.

And the energies of some passengers, disgusted at the crude behavior of the belligerent driver, bunched up also. Many fumed and swallowed lots of choking disgust

Normally, somebody in the maxi would call out to a driver behaving like that and say something like, "*Nah* man, you can't treat the gentleman like that".

Or fearing direct confrontation, but too disgusted to let an ugly scene like that pass without a word, some passengers might grumble and loudly say to no one in particular, "But the man didn't know the door would slam so hard."

Another passenger might loudly grumble to himself, "How the man would know how to close the door. If you going to be hoggish about passengers slamming doors, you should paint a sign saying, 'Don't slam'. How you could just put out a passenger like that? This country have some real hogs behind the driver's wheel, yes."

This evening, however, even the most loud-mouth youths sitting in the back of the vehicle were keeping their mouth shut. That old man driver was real *dred*, and might just put out anyone who dared question his authority to put out who he wanted to put out from his maxi.

Luckily for the ousted man, he had lots of emotional resilience, and did not allow his energies to be drained or misdirected, by the twisted up energies of the driver.

He didn't grumble, curse, or fume, or *set up his face* for everyone to see that he was very upset. And he did not make any threats. But he felt very amazed at the rude response he got that day as he waited to become once more, an integral part of his home society.

That incident, however, didn't have to end so.

## *Story #7. Ending Differently*

The gentleman had a lot on his mind. He was trying to get himself resettled and get his business started. He waited in the midst of the busy junction, on transportation. The privately owned maxi came along and stopped in front him. He was about to get on when he realized that the driver was addressing him.

"Sir," the driver said, "please pull in the door gently, after you get in."

"Oh, okay. Thanks for telling me."

"Some people slam the door so hard they spoil the lock in no time."

"Oh. Okay. Thanks again for telling me. Some drivers tell me to pull in the door hard. I won't want to slam a door when it should not be slammed."

"Coming to think of it, I'd better paint a sign on both doors. Sometimes I get real vexed when people slam my door, but as you said, people won't know which doors to slam and which doors to close gently unless we tell them.

"Yes, I think I'll paint on a sign saying, 'Please close gently'. I'll attend to that right away."

# Note 7

*The gentleman could feel happy to be back home in a country where drivers are courteous. And the driver could enjoy driving his passengers to their destination without in any way interfering with their level of personal comfort when all they want from him is to be taken without physical interference or emotional disturbance, to their desired destination for the pre-established fare.*

# STORY #8
# Unjust Maxi Attack

◆ ◆ ◆

The young man got on the privately owned mini bus, popularly called a maxi taxi, or just maxi, for short. He was one of several passengers.

The driver was in a hostile mood but the passengers had no way of knowing about the driver's emotional problems.

It wasn't their business anyhow what mood the driver was in, or even if he suffered from mood swings.

The public had an unwritten contractual arrangement with all these maxi-taxi drivers. They would get on the vehicle and get off at their desired destination for a specific well publicized, publicly advertised, well known fare.

It was the government's responsibility to ensure that only emotionally fit drivers were licensed.

The majority of maxi taxi drivers were very courteous, although some of them were fed up with some passengers who would try to avoid paying the just fare.

Drivers sometimes hired conductors to collect fares while in transit, to avoid being *ripped off*.

Many drivers made allowances for the dishonest passengers, knowing that most passengers were very honest.

Sometimes when there was no conductor on the maxi, some passengers (and these would be a very small minority of commuters) would, on reaching their destination, get off the maxi, go to the front window and hand the driver a fare less than the stipulated amount, and just boldly walk off.

It was no secret throughout the country that many drivers were disgusted with the unscrupulous behavior of these passengers, some of them, mere teenagers, and some, adults.

So the good-natured, tall, chubby young man, returning home after a stint of physical exercise a few miles away from home, rode along that night with the other passengers, through quiet foothill neighborhoods till he reached his destination.

His mom, dad, brothers and sisters, waited at home, anxious to have the one member of the family still out, arrive home safely.

It was after nine p.m.

The driver, unknown to the passengers, was brooding and seething over whatever from his array of experiences had thrown him into a very angry mood that night.

He was a ticking time bomb.

It is a task for some of these drivers to always remember where a passenger boarded their vehicle.

Sometimes you, the passenger, after looking the driver in the eye on boarding the vehicle, would feel certain that he or she must of course remember exactly where you boarded the maxi. But the driver's mind is not always where passengers might think it should be.

The young man, who had traveled a distance he thought cost two dollars, and not two fifty, or three dollars, got off the maxi.

He handed the driver the two-dollars fare and walked back a few steps along the pavement, before crossing the almost deserted night-time street to head down the dimly lit road to home with Mommy, Daddy, brothers and sisters.

Although it was getting late, the young man felt safe. This was a lonely road. But it was the only one leading to home. It was lonely because most residents in the neighborhood drove, or if they were too young to drive, they would walk only when no one at home was available to give them a ride.

After a late evening at the gym, the soft-spoken young man looked forward to an enjoyable walk home. Plugging in his earphone, he turned up the volume on his favorite tunes as he started his stroll to home.

The other passengers saw him hand the driver the two dollars. They had also remembered, as some passengers often do, exactly where he had boarded the vehicle.

The brooding driver, his face looking sour—bordering on hostile—thought of the three times that day that some passenger had cheated him out of the full fare.

He was determined that the next cheating passenger would not get away.

Some drivers say it is mostly young men who try to get away without paying the full fare.

One driver complained however, that after four months of driving maxi, he found it was mostly women who try to get away with paying less than the full fare.

And as some drivers have discovered, some of these people would be so bold, they would pay the short fare, and just walk off, with an attitude.

One maxi driver had once gone after a youth who had disembarked and coolly strolled off without paying. The driver had stepped out of his maxi. He called out to the young man telling him he needed to pay the full fare. But the youth and his friends had turned around, attacked, and murdered the driver right there outside his maxi, filled with passengers.

"That scamp not getting away tonight," the driver brooded as he eyed the young man calmly crossing the street.

Again, he glanced at the money just handed to him—just two dollars!

"This fellah thinks he is getting away, but he is mistaken", the driver dialogued in his head. But then he reflected, "This fellah handed me two open dollar notes. Those other guys who cheated me today, all handed me a folded single dollar note, and by the time I had unfolded it, those scamps were gone. Where did I pick up this fellah?

"I sure I picked him up way back there.

"He should pay me three dollars. Scamp! He not getting away with this.

"No passenger is going to get away with paying me a short-fare when they owe me for a longer distance. Not tonight. Nobody cheating me tonight".

Seething, he glared again at the young man casually strolling across the dimly lit road, peacefully heading towards home and warmth.

Medium height, and husky, the middle-age driver swiftly eased out from behind the steering wheel, on that dark, almost deserted stretch of the road, leaving his passengers momentarily stranded in the vehicle with the engine running.

The young man had no cause to look back. He had paid his honest fare, and was headed home to family and love.

The other passengers in the maxi, watched horrified, not understanding what was happening as the husky bodied driver, a man old enough to be the boy's father, dashed across the road and like a mad dog, lunged at the boy.

Confused, the tall, chubby lad felt a blow that threw him to the ground. What it was he did not know.

Why somebody was on top of him, he could not tell. He just knew that something was hitting against his back again and again.

As quickly as he had left the vehicle the driver returned, threw in the gear and with heart pumping rapidly, and breathing coming heavily, sped off even as the young man struggled to rise up from the blows.

"But the boy had given the man the correct fare", the passengers, horrified to be driven the rest of their journey with the violent chauffeur, said among themselves. "How he could just like that, rush out and attack the people's son. This is a mad man!"

"Lord", a mother turned to her teenager sitting next to her, "please get us home safely tonight." And the teenager silently nuzzled up against her mother's arm, trembling.

Meanwhile, the youngster dragged himself off the road, to the sidewalk. Terrified that whoever attacked him might return to empty his pockets, he tried to get to his feet.

The horrified passengers had no way of knowing that the violent chauffeur was not just raining fist blows on the young man's back. Looking back as the maxi sped off, they had seen the young man trying to rise up. They had no way of knowing, till they heard of it on the news the next day that he had not succeeded in rising back up to his feet.

The parents waited in vain for the arrival of their firstborn. His brothers and sisters waited up in vain. When they all saw him next, it was to identify his bloody body.

But it did not have to end like this—it didn't have to end so. This encounter could have ended differently.

## *Story #8. Ending Differently*

The young man presses the bell. The driver stops. The boy pays his fare of two dollars and walks off.

"Look at this," the driver fumes (*but he speaks loudly enough to be heard. He knows that the other passengers need to be alerted to any behavior that would impact on their comfort while in his vehicle*).

"He is not getting away with this! He gave me only two dollars and he should have given me three dollars."

Realizing that his memory might not be perfect, he turns to his passengers, "Didn't that boy come in way back there?"

"But the boy just got on the maxi," several passengers respond.

"The fare from there to here is two dollars," one passenger draws the driver's attention to the chart posted on the upper bus panel, right behind the driver. "Look you have the chart with the list of fares, posted right here, in your maxi."

"That young fellah didn't come in before that? I could swear he got on the maxi farther back.

"These young *fellahs* think they could make a fool of drivers. Three times today, three different young *fellahs* paid me short, and I swore to take care of the next one who walk off without paying me my full fare."

"But the boy paid you the correct fare", the passengers insist.

"Okay, if *allyuh* say so. Hah, God must be watching over me tonight yes, because what I had in mind to do to that fellah, not even God could have saved him tonight."

The driver drives off safely.

The passengers get to their homes disturbed at the quality of mentality they have to be subjected to just to get home safely. But every one of them is safe. Yet every one of them wonders what steps they could take to get that driver off the road without risking having him come after them.

The nice young man enters the open door to his parents' home and hearts, unaware of how real was the possibility that he might have never seen his family again.

There is no grief, no funeral. And for the driver, there is no court, yet . . . no jail, yet . . . no death sentence, yet. Maybe he would get help, yet.

# Note 8

*Oh how I wish I could have gone back there and undo the folly of that brooding driver, and return that lovely son to his mother, father, and siblings. But though, as far as I am aware, we can't go back, maybe we can prevent another such tragedy from happening. How people respond to stress might be their business, but when they are entrusted with the responsibility to deliver a service to the public then how they respond becomes everybody's business.*

# STORY #9
# Taking Care of Cutthroats

❖ ❖ ❖

"Come with me. I'm going for a drive."

"Okay."

"I want to show you something in town."

"Boy, with the amount of crime in this place I prefer to be indoors when night comes. But okay."

"Look at that place across the road, over there."

"That's not your friend's night club? How come around there looks so deserted. Not one vehicle on the street. I thought that nightclub was heavily patronized. Maybe the place looks deserted because this is a Monday night?"

"Yeh. They are closed on Monday nights. But the club is heavily patronized."

"I thought you and this man were supposed to be getting into some business together."

"Me? Not me with that underhand dog!"

"But weren't you getting into some investment with this man —some land development business? What happened? Why are you so angry?"

"The man is a dog, an underhand dog!"

"What about the three-hundred-acre parcel of land both of you were going to purchase jointly? You were talking about putting down a mall there . . ."

"With that underhand dog? Never!"

"What kind of man are you? Because you had a falling out with the man you are all puffed up, and calling him names?"

"I'm going to tell you something and let it stay right here between you and me."

"What? This must be very important."

"I'm going to fix this *fellah*."

"What do you mean, you're going to fix this *fellah*?"

"Look at that club house. See any windows or openings downstairs or upstairs?"

"No. The place looks like a fortress. Apart from those wide, heavy looking glass front doors downstairs there are no openings —no other doors, no windows—at least not from this side."

"They have windows and doors to the back. But that door right there is the one we are going to aim at. The whole three floors we bringing down. He wouldn't even know what hit him. Before he could catch himself his whole Caribbean renowned club would be demolished and scorched—that bastard! He thinks he alone could play?"

"What is all this about? I thought you and this man were getting together to buy that large parcel of land to put down a mall . . . What happened to that arrangement?"

"He got the property. That's what happened. That snake went behind my back and sealed the deal with the owners!"

"He squeezed you out? And you were the one who went to him with the idea?"

"I went to him with the proposal, not just an idea. I located that property. That property was practically mine. I invited him to invest with me so we both could make a bigger profit. That dog went behind my back and secured the property for himself, and I just found out when I went to the bank."

"I don't believe what I'm hearing!"

"He thinks he alone could play? Well, I'll show him!"

"The man is a snake—a Judas! Man, this is the worst kind of betrayal. This one is hard to take. The man is a low down dog! A real dog! He was supposed to be your friend! I could see why you're mad. What a cutthroat! That bastard!"

"I will show him!"

"What you mean you will show him? Wait, what you planning to aim at that window? You said you will demolish all three floors. What you planning to do, boy?"

"I wouldn't be doing anything."

"You would hire somebody to torch his club?"

"He'll get what he deserves."

"And you think he deserves to die?"

"If I wanted to kill that double crosser I would scorch his mansion, not his club house. But if he gets trapped in the conflagration, I won't lose one minute of sleep over him—that Judas Iscariot, that scoundrel!"

"Where people does get that kind of mind from, boy? How anybody could live with themselves after doing something like that? O God, this is hard to take. I could understand how you could feel like bringing that bastard right down—how you could want him to lose everything, to grovel."

"Trust me. He is not getting away with this."

"Wait, wait. Wait, boy. Wait. I know this is hard to take. God knows, right now I *and all* feel betrayed. I think you and I feeling the same way right now. But boy, we have to take a deep breath and pull ourselves together. We have to pull ourselves together, and allow ourselves to think clearly. Yes, the bastard is a betrayer. O Mother of God, he is a Judas. But if you set his club house on fire with patrons in it, what will that make you? Think, boy. Think. You really want to be an arsonist, and a murderer? Is that what you are? As hard as this is to swallow, think—you ever double-crossed anybody?"

"Woman, this is not about me double-crossing. This is about that Judas double-crossing me."

"So, whoever happens to be in the club house whenever you scorch it, you killing them also?"

"Nobody said anything about killing anybody."

"So who is to say who would be in those rooms when the fire starts? You could live with yourself if you wipe out all those people?"

"People die every day."

## Story #9. Ending Differently

"Come with me. I'm going for a drive."

"Okay."

"I want to show you something in town."

"Boy, with the amount of crime in this place I prefer to be indoors when night comes, but okay."

"Look at that place across the road, over there."

"That's not your friend's night club? How come around there looks so deserted. Not one vehicle on the street. I thought that nightclub was heavily patronized. Maybe the place looks deserted because this is a Monday night?"

"Yeh. They are closed on Monday nights. But the club is heavily patronized."

"Weren't you and this man supposed to get into some business project together?"

"Me? Not me with that underhand dog!"

"But weren't you getting into some investment with this man —some land development business? What happened? Why are you so angry?"

"The man is a dog, an underhand dog!"

"What about the three-hundred-acre parcel of land both of you were going to purchase jointly? You were talking about putting down a mall there . . ."

"With that underhand dog? Never!"

"What kind of man are you? Because you had a falling out with the man you are all puffed up, and calling him names?"

"I'm going to tell you something and let it stay right here between you and me."

"What? This must be very important."

"I'm going to fix this *fellah*."

"What do you mean, you're going to fix this *fellah*?"

"Look at that club house. See any windows or openings downstairs or upstairs?"

"No. The place looks like a fortress. Apart from those wide, heavy looking glass front doors downstairs there are no openings —no other doors, no windows—at least not from this side."

"They have windows and doors to the back. But that door right there is the one we are going to aim at. The whole three floors we bringing down. He wouldn't even know what hit him. Before he could catch himself his whole Caribbean renowned club would be demolished and scorched—that bastard! He thinks he alone could play?"

"What is all this about? I thought you and this man were

getting together to buy that large parcel of land to put down a mall . . . What happened to that arrangement?"

"He got the property. That's what happened. That snake went behind my back and sealed the deal with the owners!"

"He squeezed you out? And you were the one who went to him with the idea?"

"I went to him with the proposal, not just an idea. I located that property. That property was practically mine. I invited him to invest with me so we both could make a bigger profit. Now he went behind my back and secured the property for himself, and I just found out when I went to the bank this afternoon."

"I don't believe what I'm hearing!"

"He thinks he alone could play? Well, I'll show him!"

"The man is a snake—a Judas! Man, this is the worst kind of betrayal. This one is hard to take. The man is a low down dog! A real dog! He was supposed to be your friend! I could see why you're mad. What a cutthroat! That bastard!"

"I will show him!"

"What you mean you will show him? Wait, what you planning to aim at that door? You said you will demolish all three floors . . . What you planning to do, boy?"

"I wouldn't be doing anything."

"You would get somebody to torch his club?"

"He'll get what he deserves."

"And you think he deserves to die?"

"If I wanted to kill that double crosser I would scorch his mansion, not his club house. But if he gets trapped in the conflagration, I won't lose one minute of sleep over him—that Judas Iscariot, that scoundrel!"

"Where people does get that kind of mind from, boy? How anybody could live with themselves after doing something like that? O God, this is hard to take. I could understand how you could feel like bringing that bastard right down—how you could want him to lose everything, to grovel. O Mother, this bastard must not get away with this. He must not!"

"Trust me. He is not getting away with this. I'm going to make him pay!"

"Wait, wait. Wait, boy. Wait. I know this is hard to take. God knows, right now I *and all* feel betrayed. I think you and I feeling the same way right now. But boy, we have to take a deep breath and pull ourselves together. We have to pull ourselves together, and allow ourselves to think clearly. Yes, the bastard is a betrayer. O Mother of God, he is a Judas. But if you set his club house on fire with patrons in it, what will that make you?

"Think, boy. Think.

"You really want to be an arsonist, and a murderer? Is that what you are? Well, evidently this man knows who he is dealing with. Why would he want to get in business with a man who gets rid of his enemies? He must know you very well, why he decided to go through with this one without you.

"As hard as this is to swallow, think—you ever double-crossed anybody?"

"Woman, this is not about me double-crossing. This is about that Judas double-crossing me."

"So, whoever happens to be in the club house whenever you scorch it, you killing them also?"

"Nobody said anything about killing anybody."

"So who is to say who must be in those rooms when the fire starts? You could live with yourself if you wipe out all those people?"

"People die every day."

"You could feel comfortable making love to me, or hugging your children, knowing you have so much blood on your hands?"

"What you want me to do, Woman? It is my children that blasted man cheating. He's making sure his wife gets what should be yours. I didn't do any crime. It is that man who is the real criminal. And he must pay!"

"I know he is the real criminal here . . . I know. I know. This thing is hurting me plenty too. I can only imagine how this is digging at your guts. But you could give yourself some time to get over this, and in time you could get some other investment. And we could still continue to prosper. But if you tangle up yourself with this *fellah*, that could be the end of us! That could be it for this family.

"Think, boy, if you pay to kill this man, you could look at

yourself in the mirror after that?"

"I could damn well look in the mirror after doing much more than that to that double-crosser."

"This is that Daboolai* family all over again! This is your partner, Sello**, all over again!"

"I don't know what you're talking about, *nah.*"

"That man could be in the club with his wife and children when your killers strike. If you get him but his family escapes, who would take care of their grief?

"You could pay for the grief of that man's wife and children? Eh? Because you will have to pay, you know.

"If they kill me and the children, how you think you would feel?"

"I don't know why you're getting into all of this, you know."

"Because all of this is reality. Violence doesn't end with just one act of revenge, boy. Once you get involved with revenge, it just goes on and on. It never stops. Hate is like a cancer, boy. If you don't get it out early, it spreads all through you. It gets to your family, all through your business. It gets into everything you touch and sucks your life dry.

"This man is not just a number on a board that you could just wipe off and nothing would happen, you know.

"Every time somebody is murdered, you have any idea how many people suffer? Eh? You have any idea how much pain does settle over the place and how much bad karma does spread through the criminal's family?

"Boy, even people who never heard of the victims before, suffer so much pain. It is like everybody who still has a heart gets caught up in one massive, twisting heartache—one massive, common belly-twisting pain.

"Sometimes I think even the air gets distorted. You could just feel the bad energy all around you. People who went through the same trauma before and took care of their pain, like their memory does just bring everything fresh back in their mind . . . Boy you think you really know what it is you planning to inflict on this country when you plan to go after that man

"Somebody would have to pay back for all that trauma, you know. These people who think they are getting away after they kill or pay somebody to kill, they haven't gotten away, you know."

"What you mean they haven't gotten away? People who kill walking bold and strong all about the place and though the police might suspect them, they can't do them a thing because they have no evidence against these *fellahs*. I could bloody well have that *fellah* wiped out and the police would never catch the hit men."

"You want me and your children to be paying for what you want to put this country through, boy?"

"I can't afford to go through all this drama you creating, *nah*. You could afford to talk. You don't have to work to mind the children, and to keep this family living at some decent standard."

"What I am talking about is drama, yes, but it is the real drama that we have to live with every day. You have any idea how many people's lives are turned upside down, eh, when we hear they find a charred body, or another chopped up body?

"Oh God, boy, you have any idea how much grief you would bring to this place if you go through with this evil plan? Those killers might dodge the police, but boy, a mightier power has its hand on them. The eyes of God, bright like a full moon at night and fiery as the midday sun, following them every second. They think they get away, but God is watching them, boy, and God is patient."

"Woman, killers don't care about God. All they looking for is another job—another hit job so they could get a few more lousy thousand dollars."

"They will pay, boy. Unless they turn from their wickedness and go and confess their crime and turn away from a life of crime, unless they do that, they can't hide from God, boy. You want me and the children under the curse that is on every person who wound or kill? You have any idea how light headed, and frightened, and angry, people feel under the shock, when they hear about another murder? Boy, some people can't sleep at nights, and they don't know how to function in the day, when they are reeling from the shock of another crime. I tell you even nature is affected. We could feel eeriness in the air whenever somebody gets killed. You hardly talk to me, you hardly have anything to say to the children, yet still we don't want anybody to kill you. Who you think would be in that clubhouse when your killer strikes? It could be mothers and fathers, brothers and sisters, some nephews and nieces. You have any idea how many people love this man and depend on him, despite his double crossing ways? You have any idea how many people he might be bringing joy to?

"How do you expect me to function—how am I supposed to feel—knowing that another woman like myself could lose her husband or even lose her life, by tomorrow night? And all by the hands of my husband?"

"Look, I *ent* able with all this *ole talk, nah.*"

". . . And the country—you think people would get over this thing so? You know how many people might be frightened for the rest of their lives? And about you—they would find you out, sooner or later, you know. And that curse would haunt you till your last breath!

"People keep blaming the authorities for crime, but Good Lord, who in authority could know what you planning in your heart here tonight? But they would find out, boy. People talk."

"You're saying you would talk?"

"Me? I'm not talking about me. The law enforcement people are not fools. They would find out that the bank told you about this man today. They would find out that you were squeezed out of a business deal.

People aren't fools, boy. Your hired assassins would talk. These guys like to boast about their crimes. It's like a feather in their cap, I hear."

"That will be no problem. That is already taken care of."

"What? What is already taken care of? You taking a page from the book of whoever had Sello** killed? Talk on the street is that whoever ordered the hit had the assassins hit.

96

"You will kill the assassins yourself? Because whoever you get involved in your evil plot would certainly talk at some time. Just as you confide in me, they have somebody to confide in too. And I tell you, the universe brings its own justice.

"Crime does not pay, boy! Crime does not pay!

"Criminal minds have to suffer in ways you and I might never even dream of.

"Crime does not pay. Once you get involved in violence, the consequences keep going on and on, you know.

"Look how these assassins always getting assassinated. Crime does not pay. So, what is it you are really after?"

"Respect."

"And you honestly think you would get respect after killing all the people who could be in that club house when your hit man strikes? You truly, honestly think you would get respect? Why would anybody give you respect after this unless they know that you were responsible? Boy, you won't get any respect. You would feel haunted for the rest of your life. Bad karma would hound you till you and your bloody hands *hit the dust* too.

"You know who got respect after Sello's assassination? If you know then you owe it to all of us to go to the police with that information. All you hear is a set of rumors. You see anybody get charged yet for that assassination? Unless you're looking for respect from people in organized crime, I don't know what you're talking about. And once the law finds out that you are responsible, what do you think would happen? I would be taken from my comfortable home and put in jail for knowing about this plot before the fact and not reporting it. You would be put in jail for the rest of your life, unless the government finds some way to legally break your neck or poison you, or shock you to death. You would be just a corpse, boy, a living corpse or a real corpse. Then what would happen to our children? You know what they say—the sins of the fathers fall on the children, down through the generations.

"You're talking about respect. Who would respect your children? And you really think your children would ever be safe?

"You think if you wipe out somebody's family nobody would try to wipe out yours—unless you're thinking of hiding us away for the rest of our lives?"

"I'm doing this for the children."

"For the children? Haven't you heard one word I have said?

"You don't see how all kinds of strange tragedies befall some families sometimes. Sometimes, years after some people do their crime, their grandchildren still paying for it. You think that is all by chance? Who knows if it's not a case of children paying for the sins of their parents?

"Boy, this universe balances out everything.

"Vengeance belongs to God. Leave this alone and watch and see how this man would pay for double-crossing you, and you could in time forget this, and go on to prosper more.

"You found that property, why you think you can't find another one? And you might be blessed because he took that property off your hands—who knows? Let time balance out things. Get involved, and watch and see how you would pay for the rest of your life, for taking matters into your own hands.

"Look, please don't put any curse on my children. Please, I beg you."

"So you don't think it is worth it?"

"Boy, crime doesn't pay. It never pays. It just tangles up your life with bad karma."

"So what I must do, just turn my back? This thing is sticking in my craw. I just can't walk away from it."

"Then call a meeting with the man."

"What?"

"Call a meeting with the man, and leave the rest to me."

"A meeting? This man is a cutthroat. You know how many people he must have killed already. He would laugh in my face if I ask him to meet with me. All he cares about is accumulating more and more money at anybody's expense."

"We have to start doing things differently. That man is scared right now. He knows what he has done. He doesn't know what you might do. He has to be scared about you, and scared of the petty executioners running like mice, all around the place. He crossed you. He has to be feeling anxious all now. He can't be feeling safe."

"That man would pay to knock me off in a wink. He is not afraid of me."

"I tell you people like this man are running scared right now.

They don't want to be always looking under their dashboard, or in their shadow to see if somebody is after them.

"He would come, if you call a meeting, as long as he knows it is not a set-up, and he would listen. If he knows I am with you he would feel safe. Tell him I will be there. Tell him I asked for the meeting."

"Scared men could be dangerous, you know. He could set me up and say I attacked him."

"I don't think so. Everybody is tired of the killings. You are not some ignorant thug, who has to reach for a weapon because you don't have the intelligence to talk through a big problem. You are supposed to be an intelligent man, a highly respected businessman. It is time to put down guns, knives, and firebombs. It is time to stop the hostility, to give the environment a chance to heal, a chance to respire. People need some time to catch their breath, man. It is time for people in this country to start sitting together and talking out their differences like civilized reasonable people. You are going to meet with that man, and I am coming with a conflict resolution facilitator who could help both of you say what is on your minds."

"And you think that will make me feel better?"

"Any kind of understanding between you and this man would ease the tension, and make you feel better. It might take days, but we will stay with the process until you can move on from here. You could call the man all the names you want to call him in front the facilitator. You could even cuss him out if that would make you feel better. But you are going to talk, both of you."

"How you expect me to cuss in front the facilitator."

"All she cares about is that you both get talking about getting back to fairness in this transaction. Whatever it takes to offload what's on your mind, she will allow."

"Woman, I don't care about offloading my mind. What I want is to stop that bastard from *tiefing* my project. I have all the documents proving I located the land and negotiated with the previous owners for a price. I have copies of letters I wrote that man inviting him to partner with me. All I want is to regain access to the land, or buy it from this backstabber at the same price we were both going to buy it for. I could take this man to court, but that will take too long. Right now, I just want to hit this man where it will hurt the most."

"Revenge won't bring you any long lasting satisfaction. What you want is justice, and to get rid of that resentment piling up inside you. The facilitator has only two rules."

"What rules?"

"No physical intimidation or violence, and no walking out."

"How long this will take?"

"It will be up to you and the man. She will stay with you both all day and all night—all week—if necessary, if that is what it will take to bring the two of you to a mutually acceptable decision. You might have to meet again to talk some more, but we have to start at some time, and that time, I think, should be now."

"What I want is to get back inside that investment."

"I think you could still be part of that deal if you want to."

"You really think so?"

"Yes. That's the whole purpose of this meeting, to restore justice. I've seen this process work right here in this country."

"Wait a minute, who will pay for this facilitator?"

"You."

"Me?"

"Yes. It will be less costly than the cost of revenge though, and also less costly than a court case."

*Daboolai (refers to the gruesome murder of a Trinidad family a few decades ago.)

**Sello (A former Attorney General of Trinidad and Tobago whose assassins' assassination allegedly promptly followed Sello's)

END

# ABOUT THE AUTHOR

## Eugenia Springer

About the Author A former university lecturer in Biology (in the Caribbean and in the US), the author, a citizen of Trinidad and Tobago, in her own search for self-understanding, became a radio and newspaper family life counselor and an Internet Counselor in abusive relationships. Always passionate in her desire to understand what self and relationships are about and no less passionate about spilling her internal dialogues onto paper, Eugenia published her first two books, at age forty, in 1980. Girl, It's All About You, a guidance book for adolescent girls, was published by Review and Herald Publishers; and Words of a Caribbean Woman, a collection of poetry, was self-published. In her seventies, Eugenia published her first novel, a revised version of a couple of her earlier publications, and several other new titles, including the folktale, What's Up With That Dawg?! Eugenia is an alumna of the University of the Southern Caribbean (formerly Caribbean Union College) High School, in Trinidad, T&T, West Indies; and Howard University, Washington, D.C. She is also a former student of Oakwood College (now Oakwood University), Huntsville, Alabama. A mother of three, Eugenia has grand-mothered ten.

# BOOKS BY THIS AUTHOR

## Communication For Survival/It Didn't Have To End So; It Could Have Ended Differently!

"Communication For Survival/It Didn't Have to End So" tells nine illustrative stories of interactions in our homeland that ended unpleasantly or tragically because of the quality of communication between those involved. After each story, I rewrite the story showing how a different quality of communication could have changed the outcome.

We need to help our people learn to sort out their problems without violence. This is what "Communication For Survival/It Didn't Have to End So!" does.

## Words Of A Caribbean Woman (Poetry)

Eugenia captures in poetry the rhythm of her Caribbean people
" . . . Who'll sing for us
When youth is gone?
Who'll voice our sentiments
Who will carry on?    ...Excerpted from Poetry of Eugenia A. Franklin-Springer
Age has come so quickly
It doesn't seem quite fair

That so few of us have lived our dreams
All those precious dreams
Of yesteryear.

## Tantie Pearlie's Funeral

Fiction built on real life events
Tantie Pearlie's Funeral/ Fiction built on True Life events
A story of a village street community in the nineteen fifties. Through the vivacious life of the character, Pearlie, her suspicious sickness, the funeral sermon, and burial, is sensed the togetherness of the St. Michael Road people as they looked out for one another while following all the cultural funeral traditions and rituals passed down to them by the 'older heads'.

## Family Relationships/Dear Dr. Springer

Former radio and newspaper family life counselor responds to questions about love, marriage, communication, trust, parenting, self-esteem issues, infertility, STD's, and other reproductive issues, abuse, crime, and much more.

## Girl And Her Therapist

In Parts One and Two of this volume, "Girl and Her Therapist", the author uses psychodrama to present the nightmarish horror of the person violated. Rather than abandon the violated to despair, she arouses in the character a realization of her innate power to confront the problem and bring it to a resolution. In Part Three of this volume, the author embraces all bogged down in guilt and shame and points out the path to freedom. Within the covers of this book is a challenge to any laboring under the pain of self-loathing and shame, to release the shame and reclaim their power to make of their life what they will. And this challenge is also extended to any now bogged down with guilt and remorse for having in the past been a perpetrator. or an abuser.

## Soucouyants In Triniland/Wrong And Strong

Raj Dindial, a young Indian businessman has been fraudulently awarded the government contract to establish kidney dialysis treatment centers in the country of Triniland. Determined to wrest the contract from Dindial, Julia Gordio, a female drug lord with direct links to the middle-eastern community, has Dindial snatched and held in the forest till she retrieves the contract which rightfully belongs to her conglomerate.The reluctant but cooperative kidnappers are black businessmen recruited by Julia. Initially directed to hold Dindial for just a couple days, the kidnappers are subsequently ordered to execute Dindial, an order, unfolding events reveal, tantamount to being ordered to dig their own graves.___Soucouyants in Triniland/Wrong&Strong, is a work of fiction. bit too sure of herself? And if the bloke is not deceased, could her power and wealth protect her from the simple man?

## The Spiritual Journey/Gethsemane
## And The Wilderness

Author describes being taken through the ego-scrubbing process of personal transformation directed by the Inner Guide
The Spiritual Journey/Gethsemane and the Wilderness is an autobiographical account of one woman's journey from fearfulness to the brink of freedom from fear.

## Abe And Lucinda/The Curse (A Folktale)

A folktale about two young lovers separated by a curse; test of endurance, and a final showdown between good and evil.

## What's Up With Dat Dawg? (Prequel To Mister Harry And The Madam)

What's up With That Dawg A prequel to Mister Harry and the Madam. Awakened by his screaming daughter in the middle of the night, Lucinda's father under the insistence of his distraught daughter, rushes to Abe's house in the bushy part of town. With forceful entry they look around and discover a house securely locked from within, but Abe is missing. From around that time, and for many years after, a strange nuisance dog wanders through remote parts of the island.

## Mister Harry And The Madam (Prequel To Abe And Lucinda)

Mister Harry and the Madam, A prequel to Abe and Lucinda. Determined to drag the beloved young church treasurer away from his teenage love, and make the younger man her husband, the woman with a foreign accent stalks Abe. In the midst of the townsfolk, she coquettishly confronts Abe, offering him wealth and a great life. Disgusted, Abe turns down the offer telling the woman she is old enough to be his mother, and he would never marry her. Unknown to the people, she is a sorceress.

## Everyone's Pocket Marriage Counselor

Everyone's Pocket Marriage Counsel/Take Care of That Marriage Through the entertaining poetic story of Leandra and Margy, the author addresses the straying husband and his flirtatious ex. In Take Care of That Marriage, in poetic style, the author guides the couple through sticky stretches of their relationship. In Going Deeper, in brief segments, the author packages individualized personal help for any spouse troubled about their relationship.

## Girl, It's All About You

Guidance book for the adolescent girl. First published in 1980.

Made in the USA
Columbia, SC
09 January 2023

75111747R00071